Worst Words,
Worst Order

Worst Words, Worst Order

A poetry collection

Kasey Worst

Skywrote
Creations
2025

Skywrote Creations
Highland, Indiana
kaseyworst.com

ISBN # 978-1-968456-00-9

Cover and photography by Kasey Worst

Typeset in Coelacanth.
Font by Ben Whitmore.

For Aaron.
I wrote faster, and got out of my own way.
Thank you.

Contents

Content note

This book contains poems about anxiety, depression, abuse, existential dread, disordered eating, and politics.
There's also cursing.

Indoor Cat

There are birds again,
Surrounding my apartment with their sweet songs.
My cat has, somehow,
Forgotten what the wind feels like on his fur.

He sits near the open, screened-in, window.
Sniffs the fresh air.

Chirps.

Beckoning the sweet,
Feathered morsels
Closer to his maw.

Through the screen,
A breeze drawn down from the lake
Rustles his whiskers.

He bolts.

Sprinting around the room
Like he's being chased by a spectral hound.
Eventually, he hides in some little cubby
To shield himself from the sensation.

Guilt hits me.

Am I depriving him,
Keeping him inside?

Locked up and away from the wind and sun?
Confused when he catches more than a whiff
Of the wild world?

Then, I remember the strays
Abandoned at my childhood farm.

The gentle ones my parents thought
Might appease my childhood wish.

Dashed instead by a busy road
Scraped up by my gagging mother.
Buried by the corner of the sandbox,
While my brother played Taps.

Or vanished in the night,
Taken by larger predators
Before we could gain the strays' trust enough
To bring them inside.

And the birds those cats would hunt, and leave
Uneaten.
Just for the pleasure of killing
Something smaller than themselves.

We lost so many swallows
Because people saw a farm,
And decided their unwanted kitten
Would find a "perfect" home
In a paint-chipped barn.

In the city, my cat climbs back to the window,
And chatters impotently at the birds
Until the wind scares him off once more.

He will get used to it,
In time.

He always does.

Next spring,
If all goes well,
He'll forget the wind again.

How to fall

Call me a klutz,
And I'll trip over my tongue
Telling you I've been this way
Since I was young.

Scabbed-up knees,
And gravel gritted palms.
Patched up with bandages,
And antiseptic balms.

Scars on my limbs
From swings and stick fights;
One under my lip
From a playground overbite.

Changed my gait
To avoid more bruises...
My soles wore out lopsided,
Rendering the attempt useless.

Only one trick
Ever helped at all:
As the world canted around me,
I had to learn how to fall.

Formative

I grew up between two childhood homes:
One on a farm, one with a lakeside view.
The farm was second generation owned;
The lake, a rental office by the dunes.

I planted walnuts, and hauled rocks from earth
Scarred by glaciers millennia ago;
Prepped prairie grass' fiery rebirth,
With every parcel of seed I would throw.

I climbed cliff-sides down to the sandy shore,
To swim, and read, and write, and listen, calm
As fresh waters ground down black iron ore.
Grains I could collect, magnet in my palm.

The love for nature these places instilled
Is not something that is easily killed.

Worst Words, Worst Order

This is not a pen name.
Yeah, surprising, I know.
I've lived with it for decades;
Have heard all the jokes.

I don't think I need to share
The Worst of them.

Learned how to wield words myself,
When I was still quite young.
Bashing people over the head
With a shield of self-deprecation.
Preemptive strikes,
Against playground-ready weapons.

There were some good laughs in there,
Intentionally self-inflicted,
To show I had a sense of humor.

School band shirts voluntarily proclaimed
That I was the WORST CORNET around.

People delight in irony.
Especially when it turns out
I'm actually good at something.
Every success prompts somebody to comment,
At least once,
On the Good, Better or Best names
They find more fitting.

Sometimes the name feels like a dare:
You, there: prove these five little letters
Do not define your capabilities.
Make us believe in your worth.

That a name, seared into you without choice,
Does not brand you with a destiny of defeat.

Coleridge might've enjoyed wrapping my name
'Round the neck of the character
In a book of Rimes.
An on-the-nose strike of gold,
Quite difficult to subvert, no matter how I try.

After all, no matter how deftly my hands may type
Out little sonnets and free verse experiments,
Or even any epics I might spend my life to hone,
My writing will always be
The Worst words, in the Worst order.

Off Balance

Did I eat today?
Define what counts as food.
A banana, and tea, washed down vitamins
That rounded out breakfast, so...that's good?

A bowl of chips, but not a whole bag,
Sustained me through till lunch;
Reheated spaghetti, cooked the night before,
Was an efficient meal to munch.

A pricey large coffee, for an afternoon treat,
At my favorite cafe.
I only splurged after an hours-long walk
On quite the beautiful day.

Not my best dinner, I'll openly concede.
Popcorn does not fill me much.
Maybe the can of peaches I added
Will be enough to get me to brunch?

Rewire

Bathroom scales are banned from my apartment.
Same goes for cook books based on fad health trends.
No diet concoctions fill compartments
Better suited for carbohydrate friends.

I noticed a problem, back in school.
A rush to measure, many times a day.
I assured my friends they were beautiful,
Then went home, and willed my thighs away.

My favorite fruits became "calorie packs,"
As my mind gave in to propaganda.
It took some time to break guilt around snacks,
And force my health back to top agenda.

Now, sometimes, I simply forget to eat,
But I can savor a simple, sweet treat.

Do Not Feed

I have better things to do today
Than argue with a stranger online.
They will not listen to what I say.
I know it's a waste of time.

But wow, that take was heinous,
And nobody's saying a peep.
I really shouldn't do this,
I should just go to sleep.

But what if I find the perfect words
To make them understand?
What if, this time, I'll be seen and heard,
And make them change their plans?

The message sends. I hold air in my lungs,
Hoping the discussion will be fruitful.
But I might as well have written in tongues,
The way they rage like a slapped bull.

Before I know it, hours have passed,
Rebuffing and refuting.
Conveying truths and checking the facts
And dreading every ping.

How do I end the feedback loop,
Without them claiming victory?
They're still wrong, and jumping through hoops
They claim not to even see.

Maybe they are just a troll,
Cackling at my bafflement.
Surely that's how they twist and roll
Past any valid argument?

That has to be it, I tell myself,
And force my hand from the keyboard.
Nothing I say is going to help,
If the responder is simply bored.

Did I really devour all that bait?
Was this seriously all a jest?
I crawl in bed, far, far too late,
And force my mind to rest.

Estranged

Last time we spoke,
I thought it went well.
But that was two years ago,
And now I can't help
But wonder what I did
That made you walk away?
I thought we'd be friends,
Till our last dying days.

Did I call you the wrong name?
Did I trip on my tongue?
Was it just not the same
As when we were young?
Did I make your wife jealous,
Or was I just weird?
Am I overreacting?
Is there nothing to fear?

I wish I could tell you
How much it would mean
To pick your bright brain
For all that you've seen

In the time that has passed
Since you last answered my texts.
So I hope we'll speak again,
Before whatever comes next.

Wasted breath

Do not try to flirt tonight, please, stranger.
My lack of interest's not a silly game.
Nothing you say will cause me to concur
With your assumption that I feel the same.

There's no playing hard to get in my life.
I'm simply uninterested in you.
There's no judgment in that; no need for strife.
My mind simply has other things to do.

The people I have sometimes fallen for,
As few throughout the years as they have been,
Were brilliant in ways that made my heart soar...
But only once they were long valued friends.

I'm still finding who I am meant to be,
But never doubt that person is quite free.

No AI Allowed

Sometimes it's a struggle for a stanza.
Forcing my fingers to type
Anything worth the time it takes to read and write.

But stopping has never been an option.

I have trouble speaking sometimes,
When my anxiety kicks in.
Stuttering and mumbling
Through simple interactions,
Certain I'll be misinterpreted,
Even when I compose my thoughts carefully.

I used to say "I write how I speak,"
But that was never quite true.
I write how I think,
And how I wish I could be understood.

When I sit down with my thoughts,
I can take my time.
Sift through the silt of self-doubt,
And judgmental eyes,
To write out what I believe,
As clearly as I know how.

There are no awkward pauses.
There are no slurred together phrases
That muddy my meaning.

Only my truth.
Only my voice.

Why would I ever give that up?

Why would I ever allow
An algorithm to supplant my expression?

Why would anyone?

I'm not the best writer in the city,
Let alone this fragile, warming globe.
I don't expect I'll ever have enough fans
To outnumber those cooling the computers
Churning out slop from stolen works.

But at least these words are mine.

They're mine.
They're mine.
They're mine.

Expectation vs. Reality

They said she was a fighter,
So up she got
Down from her tower
Ready or not.
She wasn't afraid
To stir up the pot.

...God, I wish she were me.

Soap

My fingerprints are furrowed
With scars of cracked skin,
Formed over decades
From the soap I was given.

Worst in the cold months,
Woodstove sizzling hot,
But always present in some measure,
When'er I drew the dishwashing lot.

Every bowl, cup and plate
Cleaned, always, by hand.
No room in the farmhouse kitchen
For a dishwasher, expensive and grand.

It took me time to realize
The connection 'tween the suds,
And the way my fingers peeled and split
To shed more than a little blood.

I tried hard to explain it
To the one who tasked my chores,
But he said I was full of shit,
And to go vacuum the floors.

My hands are all healed up now,
But scars remain where the detergent cleaved.
Divots left forever to remind me
What it's like to not be believed.

Hysteria

There is a vaccine
To prevent certain cancers
With nothing more than a couple pricks.

Folks called it obscene
When it first hit the headlines.
My conservative neighbors screamed:
"It will make girls into sluts!"
With no evidence;
Simply self-righteous judgment,
And zero regard
For the long-term protections provided
By a couple, simple jabs.

I received the vaccine anyway.
Because my mother loved me enough
To value wiping a slate of cancers from my future
More than social stigma.

Now, here I am.
A single woman,
In my thirties,
Fully vaxxed by this "sinful" solution
Since my teens.

Want to hear the details
Of how this devious concoction
Hijacked my personality
And destroyed my innocence?

Well, here you go:

In the well over decade
Since my fateful pricks,
I've had quite the...
Nontraditional
Love life.

Ready for the shock?
You sure?

Don't want your Puritan heart
Swooning on me.

Alright, I warned you:

In all this temptuous time,
Not a single romantic tryst,
Or even a partner,
Has even gotten past a kiss.
And those were kind of boring.

Just not really my thing, I guess.
Never has been.
Not sure it ever will be.

So I have to wonder,
After all the outcry and rage
Over a literal life-saver:
When is the "unsavory" side effect
Of this supposedly devilish drug
Supposed to kick in?

Judge Not

I want my loved ones safe
From ignorant, self-righteous fury.
From those who use the very same breath
To claim revelation,
And condemn.

Why is that so difficult to achieve?
Why does this history once again repeat?
Why can't grace overcome judgmental fear
Among so many who believe?

Despair

How does one plan for a future
Rapidly turning to ash?
Do I run back to the family farm?
Do I bury all my cash?

What fruits can I bear that will matter
As carbon chokes the skies,
And precious preserves are ripped apart
To postpone stock market dives?

I want to believe in better;
That there's a way to turn this around.
I pray that we will find it
Before the last of our species is in the ground.

Not Weird, "Unique."

I think I finally understand
Why I never outgrew
The constant humming...
And occasional flapping of hands...
That were barely tolerated
When I was small enough to be cute.

I used to see exhaustion
In other people's eyes,
And I would smile at them
Thinking, somehow,
That would be enough
To make their spirit come alight.

Instead, they accused me of frowning,
Which I didn't understand.
I felt myself smiling.
How was I not smiling right?
So I practiced faces in the mirror
To make expression mine to command.

I was outspoken
In ways people disliked.
But what else was I supposed to do?
Let those boys blab bullshit
'Bout their edgelord fantasies
That women don't deserve rights?

I chalked it up to their conservative views
When those children turned to bullies.
I thought the right words, said sure enough,
Were all I needed to change them.
But now I think I misunderstood
The barrier between them and me.

Even my friends would call me weird,
But it was a badge I wore with pride.
Everyone, after all,
Is weird in their own way.
So why should I be ashamed of that?
Why is it a reason to hide?

My mother delighted
At the connections my mind made.
But worried when I called myself strange.
"You're just unique," she'd say lovingly.
"A brilliant, complex mind,
far wiser than your age."

A sentiment full of care,
That I still appreciate.
Though I have to wonder
If I could've coped better in college
Had I understood myself more clearly
Before it was time to graduate.

Now, I attempt to control the sounds around me
Whenever I need to think.
I still touch the walls and chirp bat calls,
And my skin crawls over anything sticky.
And though tests can be done,
I'm unsure I want to know
If there's more to it than simply being "unique."

Trying for better

The world I want's not built on perfection:
A liminal lie no one can achieve,
No matter exterior perceptions
That elevate internal biases.

The world I want is miles from callous:
It strives for kindness, fairness and mercy,
As guards against any unchecked malice
Fearful good intentions might not foresee.

The world I want cares about the future:
Sturdy trees planted in places they thrive.
Habitats mended with careful suture,
Ensuring Earth stays vibrant, and alive.

Hope for that world is what keeps me writing,
In this tinderbox, close to igniting.

Two Steps Forward,
Six Decades Back

My mother once lived where a river caught fire
From chemicals companies dumped down its banks.
Restaurants used to choke with second hand smoke
Invading infants' lungs, and everything stank.

Dust billowed across the country
In drifts that smothered the sun.
And lead-lined exhaust poured, grey and gasping
From blackened pipes whenever a car would run.

Then, laws changed.

Regulations passed,
To save ourselves from greed.
We hoped it would last.

Businesses blocked from poisoning streams.
Smokers made to puff outside.
Cropland protections put in place.
Gas reformulated to ease every ride.

It was not an overnight process.
It was stop and start.
Decades of progress.
Millions doing their part.

I've never had to watch a river burn.
I haven't gagged in a restaurant since twenty-ten.
I've been in a small dust storm,
But nothing like from Way Back When.

The gas in my car, though still carbon-coughing,
At least does not fill my neighborhood with lead.
And I can sleep far easier
Without asbestos above my bed.

So why would anyone ever want to return
To poisoned rivers and polluted skies?
How does anyone with a soul
Put profits above human lives?

Low point

I'm finding it hard to keep pretending
That everything's okay.
Inspiration all around me,
But I don't know what to say.

Sure, writing's cheaper than therapy,
But my hands are getting sore.
And I've no idea who I'd be
If I couldn't write anymore.

Seriously, Brain?

I will put fresh sheets on the bed
The moment I get home.
I will not get distracted.
I will not sleep on bare foam.

The dishes will be done
In a timely manner.
Nothing will mold
On pot, pan or platter.

My laundry will not mildew
In a long forgotten heap.
An organized closet
Is a reward I can reap.

The floor will be vacuumed.
The garden will be watered.
My novel will be written.
My clothing will be altered.

I promise myself all this,
And keep to it, best I can...
But if my mind wanders too far.
I'll sleep on bare foam again.

Collateral

If the sand between my toes
Ever turns to glass,
I hope it's from a lightning strike.

Quick.

Precise.

Nobody else around me
Close enough to feel
The bolt gallop through their bodies.

Deadly.

Contained.

At least then, in the fallout,
No radiation
Will bother the nesting turtles.

Buried.

Waiting.

But Alive.

Do I really have to say this?

No, empathy is not the enemy.
Kindness does not diminish one's true might.
Wise minds know when it's best to show mercy,
Not beat and belittle those who can't fight.

What purpose does it serve to be cruel
To those who simply want to live their lives
A little differently than what you know?
Why does the thought break you out into hives?

Do not give me those tired excuses
Of Tradition wielded like a cudgel.
Knowing the past can have potent uses,
But other's paths are not yours to control.

You cannot espouse love for Liberty,
And spit in the face of Diversity.

Affirmations

I will not spend all day inside.
I will not crawl away and hide.
I will not surrender my only voice.
I will not let fear steal my choice.

I can make a difference if I try.
I was not born just to work and die.
There's so much left I get to see.
I am allowed to just be me.

In-Law

Hey Patrick,
You hate it
When I break the Fourth Wall,
Right?

And obsolescent dialogue
Irks you tremendously.
You vastly prefer when well-parsed phrases
Replace pretentious pattering.

Good to know.

Or should I say,
What advantageous intelligence to acquire.

I know I'll pay for this,
The next time
I settle down
At your welcoming game table.

But what's family for,
If I can't tease a little?

What I Needed to Hear

I used to fantasize
That somebody would see
Everything I hid away,
And then I would be free.

Nobody's gonna ask
The perfect question to reveal
Your hidden, special talent,
To knock them on their heel.

Hate to tell ya this,
Most people can't read minds.
So don't hold yourself back,
Waiting for some rod to divine.

It takes time.
It takes skill.
It takes so much freaking effort,
Both ways, uphill.

But no matter what volume you shed
Of blood, sweat, or tears,
None of your work will change a thing,
If you hide it away in fear.

Repeat, Repeat, Repeat

Screaming it louder
Doesn't make it true.
Better to stay calm,
And think of a way through.
Following this mantra
Is how I won't become you.

Glass houses

My family loves to tell
The story of Uncle Frank:
A teen refugee from Czechoslovakia,
Who fled to the teeming shores of America
After killing three murderous, rapist soldiers
Who thought their power made them untouchable.

His family gave all they could spare
To spirit him towards freedom.
They could not afford a cabin,
So he had to sleep with the mail,
Postage pinned to his shirt.

The story is told with awe at his spirit.
That drive to survive and persevere,
Even in the absolute worst of times,
When all but hope must be abandoned.

Which is why I am disgusted, every time
Those same holders of history decry modern refugees
As dangerous killers, unworthy of mercy.

Or too poor, and burdensome,
To be worth granting access

To what Uncle Frank was already given.

Bubbie

My great-aunt had missing fingers
From her childhood spent in the mills.
The ends of the truncated digits
Rounded by ninety years of slow healing
That still hurt her when it rained.

I think of her,
Each and every time,
I see cash-bloated companies
Complain that they can't squeeze extra years
Of cheap labor
Out of vulnerable youth.

Family Lore

My great-Uncle Frank
Once threw Henry Ford
Into a fishing hole
Near that nazi-lover's factory
When he demanded Frank vacate
His own hard-won property
For Ford's personal use.

At least, so the family story goes.
I have my doubts.

But God,
It's a nice thought.

Hope

"How naive,"
I've been told all my years,
To push for a world
Not run by base fears.
A place where clean air
Takes priority over market share.
Where human dignity is respected
No matter how profits are affected.

It's easy
To claim that all is lost.
To give up one's hope,
And ignore the cost.
Defeatism is a curse
Made to erode and disburse
The will of those who would fight
For the things they know are right.

So, you want to talk indoctrination?

I took a tour, back in high school
Of a conservative college, close to my home.

My tour was organized as a class trip,
Not a visit of my choosing.
But I tried, as I'd been taught,
To keep an open mind.

I didn't know much, going in.
Just that my father hated the place.
Which, frankly,
Was a coin toss.

The campus was stately,
Crisp, commanding and clean.
The buildings styled
For academic luxury.

Another student, excited by the club offerings,
Asked about scholarships and grants.
The tour guide shuffled.
"Well, we don't accept those,
But if you catch an alumni's eye,
They just might foot the bill."

Many classmates deflated.
Public school kids,
The lot of us.

In a place still recovering
From the Great Recession.

I gritted my teeth,
Standing in my hole-toed shoes,
And put a hard line through the school's name
In my mental list of options.

But the tour continued,
And so I kept listening
Spotting scarlet banners
With every new "perk."

Our guide brought us to a lecture hall,
To break down their curriculum,
And the "core subjects"
They believed
Every student should study
To fully understand the world:

Western heritage.
American heritage.
Theology.

...The last of which,
By the tour guide's own admission,
Really meant The Bible.

My peers were diverse.

Some Muslim.
Some Sikh.
Mostly Christian,
But even some of them shut down
During this description.

I was and am agnostic,
And stared in disbelief
At the dismissive disrespect
This so-called place of higher learning
Espoused to my peers.

When asked about alternatives
That respected diversity of thought,
We were given a response that,
Over a decade later,
Still sends dread
Shuddering down my spine.

"Don't worry,"
The smiling student said confidently.
"You might not have our values when you come here,
But you will when you leave."

ROYGBIV

Today, the air was tinged blue,
From wildfires in Canada,
Whose smoke billowed south
To mingle with the steel mill smog
That often wafts over from the lake.

There is a silty film on my tongue.
Not gritty.
Just there.

My lungs hurt, just a twinge.
I can ignore it for now.
My cat keeps sneezing.
I hope he's okay.

Nuclear power is coming back,
But only to service machine learning centers.
The power that once lit up whole cities
Siphoned off so someone doesn't have to type out
A whole essay themselves,
Or hire an artist.

Blue air.
Last year, California's smoke
Turned the sky orange for days.

What hue does it need to be
Before people finally see
The full spectrum of our reality?

110%

I tried all the tired tropes,
But all that left behind
Was burnout and delayed dreams
That made my hopes unwind.

I'm learning to relax again
In ways that don't cause guilt.
To celebrate small successes
After everything I've built.

I'll never be that movie star
Accepting the big award.
But I still can't wait until you see
All I've been working toward.

Wetland

This refuge is not perfect.
A freeway borders the far side,
And hundreds of drowned, fallen trees
Bleach in the sun, years after they've died.

Traffic noise roars, louder than the wind.
Biting, with little left to buffer
Its force across the raised embankment,
Built to satiate the curious nature lover.

The dam that sustains the flooded lands
Did not, it seems, account for the trees' tolerance
To water, perpetual, drenching their roots.
Laying slow waste to their habitat by happenstance.

Still, as I sit here, a swallow soars overhead.
A heron perches proudly on a broken stump,
Surrounded by blue ripples and gossiping geese.
Close to the edge, frogs sing and jump.

Yes, the wetland before me could use some restoration,
But that doesn't diminish the value of its conservation.

Flickering Futures

When I'm sixty five,
Will there still be fireflies?

Will my family's farm fields still glitter
With the galaxy of little lives,
Blinking out their short summer cycles
As they have since long before
I could comprehend their novas?

Will the trees still spark like a city of fairies,
A civilization with rules which I could only dream,
Back when my child's eyes reflected back
Their bright bioluminescence?

Or will the fields be dark?
Living stars, dwarfed and dwindled
Year by year by landscaping and pesticides
Until nothing but the void of their glow remains?

Will the trees be nothing but bleak silhouettes
Against the bare moonlight?
Civilization causing the sterilization
Of a child's imagination?

When my years more than double,
And laughter and tears line my eyes,
I hope,
Oh, how I hope,
That there will still be fireflies.

Chicken Scratch

Keyboards are a blessing
With handwriting like mine.

No matter the practice,
No matter how closely I copied,
My hands have never been able to scrawl
Those smooth strokes that come so easily
To almost everyone around me.

Chicken scratch.
That's what it's called.
The way my letters jolt across the page
Jabbed into the paper
As I try to make it legible.

My teachers must have been saints
To patiently decode my essays.
When given the time,
I'd write them twice
Just to give them a cleaner copy.
...What little good that would do.

But still, I write, and write, and write.
Even if only I can decipher
My unintentional code.
And I plan to keep scratching
Far after I grow old.

Depression Can Suck It

Every word is a victory.
Every sentence a triumph.
Every paragraph, every chapter,
Screams the evidence
My mind still struggles to believe:

I'm here.
Still here, motherfucker.
And I'm nowhere near ready to go.

Quitting's not allowed

Do not write Liberty's obituary
Quite so soon.
This is not a twilight
It's high noon.

We let a wound fester
That's now turned to rot:
A tumor's metastasized,
Bigoted bile boiling hot.

What comes now isn't pretty:
Innocents already being harmed,
By a wannabe king's decrees,
With soldiers rallied and armed.

But the future's not etched
In an unyielding granite slab.
The people were not born
To pay the billionaires' tab.

Speak the truth,
As is your human right,
And never stop demanding
A future that is bright.

Aaron

Where is your obituary?

I look for it, again and again
On death-notice websites and social media
And anywhere else I can think to scour
For something as simple
As confirmation that you had a funeral.

But, still,
Nothing.

The timing makes my stomach sink.
You were days out from a trip
You'd been planning for months.
You'd earned that rest.

I'm embarrassed to say I forgot
You were taking time away.
I emailed you,
The day after you died,
When I thought you were late to our session.
Just to check in,
Since our connection had been spotty lately,
And there was a good chance
I simply needed to be more patient.

When at first you didn't email back,
I thought you'd ghosted me.

Then I remembered your trip,
And felt waves of relief.
And more than a little chagrin
Over the messages that would be waiting
When you returned.

I made myself believe it would be okay.
I just had to wait
Until I could apologize for forgetting,
And we'd laugh it off,
And everything would be okay.

Until the next week.
...And the next.

And...

Nothing.
Nothing.
Nothing.

I thought you were mad at me.
I emailed some more,
Genuinely worried,
And with no other way to contact you.

I told my brother,
Who said I was probably overthinking.
I wish he was right.

Aaron

I wish you had ghosted me.
Far better that, than the real thing.

After weeks of silence, your brother replied
On an email that once was yours.

Heart attack, he said.

The day before the first missed session.

That is all I know.
That is all I'll ever know.

He didn't reply to my condolences,
Typed out through tear-blurred eyes.
That's alright.
I know what grief feels like.
I'm grateful he told me at all.

I just miss you.
And I hate the silence you left behind.

Your church put out a short post on your passing.
The exact same info relayed by your brother.
Nothing more than that.

Nothing about a funeral.
Nothing about where to find
Even a short summary

Of the wild ride of a life
I know was yours.

You couch surfed the country.
You sang opera.
You were a deacon.
You mentored children.
You reinvented yourself
Over and over
With kindness and honesty
At the forefront of every experiment.

But now...nothing.

All I have left are questions
That will never be answered.
You'd think as an agnostic,
I'd be used to that by now.

But how the heck do I let go?
Stop scraping the barrel's bottom
To find any concrete mark of your passing?
It's there,
Somewhere.
It has to be there, right?

I don't know.
I'll don't think I'll ever know.

Aaron

Your website is gone.
Your profiles are private.
The scant evidence of your life online
Is turning to mist.

I'm trying to be okay.
Trying to maintain the tools we developed
In honest, painstaking morning talks.
I swear, I'm trying.

My mother says you were an angel.
Put here to help others,
If for a shorter time than hoped.
And you did.
I cannot write you enough words
To make it clear how much you mattered.

And even though it hurts,
I do not regret a single second
Of our conversations
Where hard truths were wrought
Hour by hour, session by session
Reconciling emotion with thought.

Heartz and Minds

I've wanted to inspire real action,
Like my namesake did, as she shaped state lands
With powerful language, pencil and pen
That influenced future caretaker's hands.

As a child, I explored wild parks
Left in the wake of her life's endeavor.
She saved natural spaces from ugly marks
Wrought by greed's temptuous call, "forever."

Now, everything she worked for is threatened
As regulations roll back like waves beached.
Eroding once-thought shored-up protections
For fragile lands, slipping fast from our reach.

I fear I'm too late, but still I will try
To champion the earth, water and sky.

Subtext

I think I'm a coward
For the pieces cut from this collection.
There's so much more to say;
So many more reflections
On all that I have learned
Through rage and joy and sorrow.
Maybe I'll find the words,
If I try again tomorrow.

Little Dreams

The cafe is covered in rainbow flags,
A preparation for the month of June.
The wall art's labeled with careful price tags
As the staff pick out their favorite tunes.

On Sunday nights, the cafe comes alive.
Crowded with contenders for a short list,
As singers, poets and musicians strive
To craft a performance that can't be missed.

I've wanted a place like this all my life
Where my friends and I could simply belong.
Where I could stay for hours, just to write
And gain the courage to burst into song.

I sip my drink, as my searching eyes gleam.
How good it feels to achieve little dreams.

Special Thanks

To my mother, Kathy, for a lifetime of support, a childhood of library visits, and the patience to hear me babble on for hours about my latest projects. I know some of the poems in this collection were hard for you to read, and I truly appreciate the feedback.

To my brother, Chris, for the funny feedback, and far more serious notes, that helped me shape the final version of this collection. Merci, mon frere.

To my brother-in-law, Patrick, for being the blunt one. I may not have taken all of your advice, but I considered every single word.

I love you all. Thank you.

Kasey Worst is a poet, writer and designer. Born and raised in Michigan, Kasey now lives in the Chicagoland region with her cat, Oscar. Worst Words, Worst Order is her debut collection, inspired by family history, personal struggles, politics and nature.

Questions?

Please contact worstkasey@gmail.com
Information about current and upcoming projects can be found at kaseyworst.com